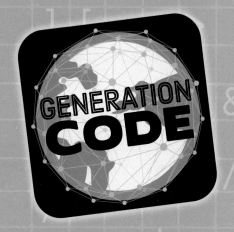

GENERATION CODE

I'M AN ADVANCED SCRATCH CODER

Max Wainewright

WAYLAND
www.waylandbooks.co.uk

CONTENTS

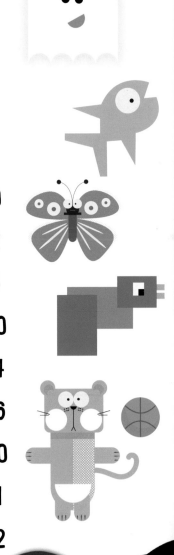

INTRODUCTION

If you know the basics of Scratch and you want to go to the next level, then this book is for you! It contains loads of great projects and ideas so you can become an advanced Scratch programmer. Learn how to make games, animate stories and write musical programs, using a range of coding techniques like loops, variables and IF statements. Once you've got things working, you can customise the programs using your own ideas and graphics.

Here is a quick reminder of the different parts of Scratch and what they do:

TRY IT OUT

Open your web browser, type in:

scratch.mit.edu

and select TRY IT OUT to get started!

File Menu (for logged-in users):
Create an account for free and save your work online.

File Menu (for general users)
Upload and download to save and open work on your computer.

Block Palette
Choose commands from a list of categories.

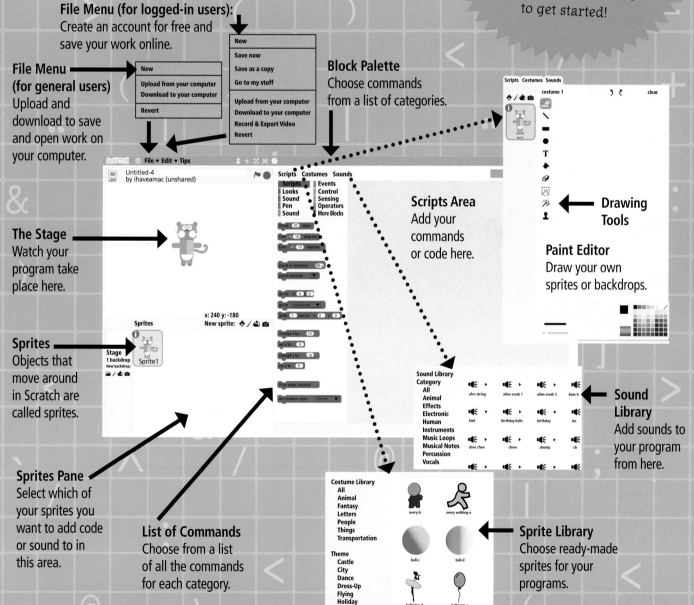

The Stage
Watch your program take place here.

Sprites
Objects that move around in Scratch are called sprites.

Sprites Pane
Select which of your sprites you want to add code or sound to in this area.

List of Commands
Choose from a list of all the commands for each category.

Scripts Area
Add your commands or code here.

Drawing Tools

Paint Editor
Draw your own sprites or backdrops.

Sound Library
Add sounds to your program from here.

Sprite Library
Choose ready-made sprites for your programs.

› GHOST STORY

In this program, we will use an algorithm to make a story using **Looks** command blocks, simple animation, sound effects and loops. The story will follow a cat in a scary building who gets frightened away by a ghost.

STEP 1 – SET THE SCENE

⇨ Click the **Stage** icon in the **Sprites Pane**.

⇨ Click the **Choose backdrop from library** icon.

⇨ Click the **hallway outdoors** image, or your own choice.

⇨ Click **OK**.

STEP 2 – ADD SOUND

⇨ Click the cat sprite in the **Sprites Pane**.

⇨ Click the **Sounds** tab.

⇨ Click the **Choose sound from library** icon.

⇨ Click **bell toll**.

⇨ Click **OK**.

⇨ Now repeat this to add two more sounds: **door creak** and **scream-female**.

CUSTOMISE

• Change what the cat and the ghost are saying.

• Try adding another character, or sprite, to the story.

• Try starting another story with different sprites.

• What will it be about?

• What will happen?

AVOID THE BUGS!

Bugs are errors or mistakes in your code that stop your program working properly. Looking for these errors is called debugging. Make sure you enter your code really carefully. If things aren't working properly, use the tips on page 31 to help you.

STEP 3 – SAY 'HI!'

⇨ In the **Scripts Area**, build the following code:

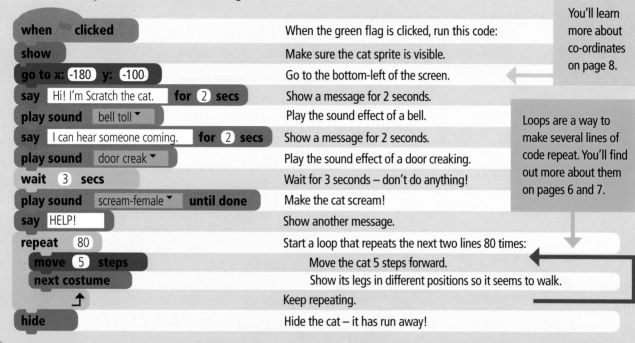

Code	Explanation
when clicked	When the green flag is clicked, run this code:
show	Make sure the cat sprite is visible.
go to x: -180 y: -100	Go to the bottom-left of the screen.
say Hi! I'm Scratch the cat. for 2 secs	Show a message for 2 seconds.
play sound bell toll ▾	Play the sound effect of a bell.
say I can hear someone coming. for 2 secs	Show a message for 2 seconds.
play sound door creak ▾	Play the sound effect of a door creaking.
wait 3 secs	Wait for 3 seconds – don't do anything!
play sound scream-female ▾ until done	Make the cat scream!
say HELP!	Show another message.
repeat 80	Start a loop that repeats the next two lines 80 times:
move 5 steps	Move the cat 5 steps forward.
next costume	Show its legs in different positions so it seems to walk.
↰	Keep repeating.
hide	Hide the cat – it has run away!

> You'll learn more about co-ordinates on page 8.

> Loops are a way to make several lines of code repeat. You'll find out more about them on pages 6 and 7.

STEP 4 – ADD A GHOST

⇨ We need another sprite for our story. Click **Choose sprite from library**.

⇨ Click **Ghost1**.

⇨ Click **OK**.

 **KEY CONCEPT**

ALGORITHM

• To make a program work properly, we need to work out all the steps we need to take and put them in the right order.

• An algorithm is a bit like a plan that helps us get all these steps correct.

STEP 5 – MAKE IT SAY BOO!

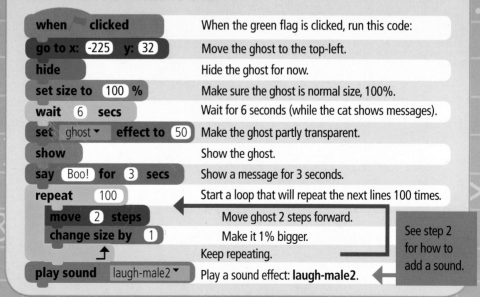

Code	Explanation
when clicked	When the green flag is clicked, run this code:
go to x: -225 y: 32	Move the ghost to the top-left.
hide	Hide the ghost for now.
set size to 100 %	Make sure the ghost is normal size, 100%.
wait 6 secs	Wait for 6 seconds (while the cat shows messages).
set ghost ▾ effect to 50	Make the ghost partly transparent.
show	Show the ghost.
say Boo! for 3 secs	Show a message for 3 seconds.
repeat 100	Start a loop that will repeat the next lines 100 times.
move 2 steps	Move ghost 2 steps forward.
change size by 1	Make it 1% bigger.
↰	Keep repeating.
play sound laugh-male2 ▾	Play a sound effect: **laugh-male2**.

> See step 2 for how to add a sound.

 Now press the green flag to check your code!

⟩ LOOPS

If you want your code to do something over and over again, it's much quicker to use a loop. The **repeat** loop in Scratch allows you to repeat some code a specific number of times. As a quick reminder, let's draw a simple square.

STEP 1 – DRAW A SQUARE ▷

```
when     clicked        When the green flag is clicked:
pen down                Put the pen down to draw when the cat sprite moves.
repeat  4               Start a loop that will repeat 4 times – one for each side:
   move  100  steps        Move the cat sprite forward 100 steps.
   turn ↻  90  degrees      Turn the cat sprite right 90 degrees.
      ↱                  Keep repeating.
```

⇨ When you run your code by clicking the green flag, you should see the cat sprite draw a square on the screen. Try to change your code to make the square bigger. Now make it smaller. Can you add more code to draw another square below it?

STEP 2 – LOTS OF SQUARES ▷

⇨ If you want to draw lots of squares, you could make another loop that fits around the first loop. After each square is drawn, it will turn the cat sprite 15 degrees before drawing the next one. Change your code so it looks like this:

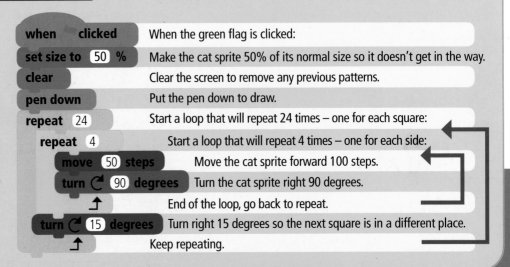

```
when     clicked        When the green flag is clicked:
set size to  50  %      Make the cat sprite 50% of its normal size so it doesn't get in the way.
clear                   Clear the screen to remove any previous patterns.
pen down                Put the pen down to draw.
repeat  24              Start a loop that will repeat 24 times – one for each square:
   repeat  4              Start a loop that will repeat 4 times – one for each side:
      move  50  steps        Move the cat sprite forward 100 steps.
      turn ↻  90  degrees     Turn the cat sprite right 90 degrees.
         ↱                End of the loop, go back to repeat.
   turn ↻  15  degrees     Turn right 15 degrees so the next square is in a different place.
      ↱                  Keep repeating.
```

When you run your code, it will draw a pattern like this – with 24 squares, each at a slightly different angle.

⇨ Look back through the code and think about what each line does. Try changing your code so it draws more squares. To stop the squares overlapping, you will need to change the angle turned after each one.

There are 360 degrees in a complete turn. So with 24 squares, the sprite has turned 15 degrees: 360 ÷ 24 = 15. For 36 squares, the sprite must turn 10 degrees: 360 ÷ 36 = 10.

CHANGING COLOUR

In the **Pen** blocks, find the **set pen color** block. Drag it into your code to change the colour of your pattern.

set pen color to

To choose a new colour, click this square, then click on a new colour somewhere on the screen.

STEP 3 – LOTS OF LOOPS ▶

⇨ Change your code by adding another loop below the first one. Use the **set pen color** block to choose a different colour for each part of the pattern.

After your code runs, you should see a double pattern like this.

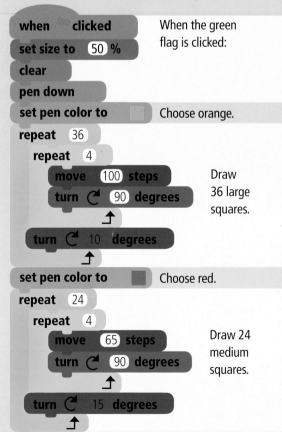

```
when  clicked              When the green
set size to  50 %          flag is clicked:
clear
pen down
set pen color to           Choose orange.
repeat  36
    repeat  4
        move  100  steps       Draw
        turn ↻  90  degrees    36 large
                               squares.
    turn ↻  10  degrees
set pen color to           Choose red.
repeat  24
    repeat  4
        move  65  steps        Draw 24
        turn ↻  90  degrees    medium
                               squares.
    turn ↻  15  degrees
```

CUSTOMISE

• Think about how you could add more loops to create a third smaller pattern in the middle.

• What colour will you choose?

⬗ **KEY CONCEPT**

THE LOOP
In coding, when we want to repeat some code, we use a loop.

 🚩 Now press the green flag to check your code!

⟩ FAST FISH

This simple game uses a conditional loop to make a fish swim down a river, using the mouse to guide it. If the fish touches the sides of the river, the game is over. The game uses a **go to** code block to set the starting co-ordinates of the fish.

STEP 1 - CHANGE THE CAT FOR A FISH ▷

⇨ Find the **Sprites Pane**.

⇨ Right-click the cat sprite and click **delete**.

⇨ Add a fish sprite by clicking **Choose sprite from library**.

New sprite

⇨ Click **Fish1**.

⇨ Click **OK**.

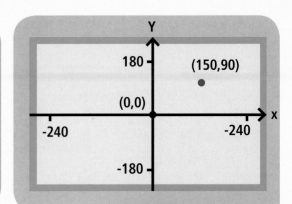

Setting co-ordinates

All sprites on the stage have co-ordinates, or **x** and **y** values. The **x** value tells us how far across the stage the sprite is. The **y** value tells us how far up or down it is.

In the example above, the command **go to x: y:** would move the blue dot sprite to a position **x: 150** steps to the right and **y: 90** steps up.

STEP 2 - GET READY ▷

when clicked	When the green flag is clicked:
set size to 25 %	Make the fish smaller – a quarter of its normal size.
go to x: -200 y: 120	Move the fish to the top-left of the stage.

⚑ Now press the green flag to check your code!

STEP 3 - DRAW A FIELD

⇨ Click the **Stage** area in the **Sprites Pane**.

⇨ Click the **Backdrops** tab.

⇨ Click the **Fill with color** tool.

⇨ Choose a green for the field.

⇨ Fill your background in green.

STEP 4 - DRAW A RIVER

⇨ Choose the **Rectangle** tool.

⇨ Choose a blue for the river.

⇨ Make sure the rectangle will be filled in by choosing the filled rectangle instead of the outline on the left-hand side.

⇨ Draw the river with a series of blue rectangles. Remember: if you make a mistake, click the **Undo** arrow.

STEP 5 - FINISH THE CODE

⇨ Click on **Fish1** in the **Sprites Pane**.

⇨ Click the **Scripts** tab. Your code from Step 2 should now appear.

```
when ⚑ clicked
set size to 25 %
go to x: -200 y: 120
point in direction 90▾
repeat until ⟨ touching color ? ⟩
    move 1 steps
    point towards mouse-pointer ▾
```

This is the code from step 2, which gets the fish to the start position and makes it smaller.

Point the fish to the right.

Repeat the following code until the fish hits green:

    Move the fish 1 step.

    Make the fish point towards the mouse cursor.

Keep repeating.

 Now test your code and enjoy the game!

KEY CONCEPT

CONDITIONAL LOOP

A conditional loop keeps repeating until something happens or changes.

> GET DRUMMING

In this next activity, we will be looking at how to use sound in Scratch. We can make a simple drum kit by adding a number of sprites and **Sound** blocks, which will play a drum rhythm over and over again.

We will use the cat sprite as a drummer and make him rotate slowly with a loop. When the sprite hits a drum, the drum will sound. By moving the drums around, we can change the rhythm and the sound that will be played.

STEP I – ADD A DRUM SPRITE

⇨ Click on **Choose sprite from library**.

⇨ Click **Music** from the list of themes.

⇨ Click the **Drum-Bass** icon.

⇨ Click **OK**.

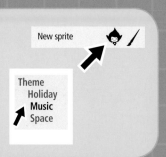

New sprite

Theme
Holiday
Music
Space

STEP 2 – MAKE IT PLAY

⇨ Add the following code to the drum sprite:

when this sprite clicked

play drum 2▾ **for** 0.25 **beats**

Run the following code when the drum is clicked:

Play drum number 2 (the bass sound) for a quarter of a beat.

⇨ Try clicking on the drum. If you can't hear anything, check your code is correct. Still nothing? Check your speakers are plugged in and turned up.

STEP 3 – ADD ANOTHER DRUM

⇨ Repeat step 1 to add **Drum1**.

⇨ Repeat step 2 to add this code to **Drum1**:

when this sprite clicked

play drums 1▾ **for** 0.25 **beats**

Run the following code when the drum is clicked:

Play drum number 1 for a quarter of a beat.

⚑ Click the flag to test your code.

STEP 4 – COMPLETE YOUR KIT

⇨ Repeat steps 1 and 2 to add **Drum2** and **Cymbal**. Experiment with the sounds and drums available. Now test your drums.

STEP 5 – TURN YOUR KIT INTO A DRUM MACHINE

⇨ Position your drums in a circle around the cat sprite.

STEP 6 – DRAW A DRUMSTICK

⇨ Click on **Sprite1** in the **Sprites Pane**.

⇨ Click the **Costumes** tab.

⇨ Click the **Line** tool. Slowly and carefully, draw a drumstick for the cat to hold. If you make any mistakes as you draw, click **Undo**.

STEP 7 – KEEP MOVING

⇨ Click the **Scripts** tab and add this code to **Sprite1**, so that the cat rotates slowly round and round.

Code	Explanation
when clicked	When the green flag is clicked:
forever	Repeat the following code forever:
turn ↻ 10 degrees	Rotate the cat right by 10 degrees.
↰	Keep repeating.

STEP 8 – BANG THE DRUMS

⇨ Click on the drums in the **Sprite Pane** and add this code to each of the drums. Remember to choose the correct drum to play. Try moving the drums around to change the rhythm.

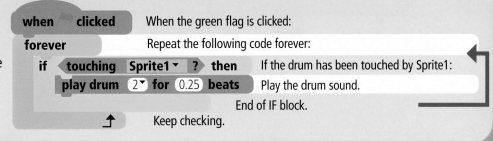

Code	Explanation
when clicked	When the green flag is clicked:
forever	Repeat the following code forever:
if ⟨ touching Sprite1 ▾ ? ⟩ then	If the drum has been touched by Sprite1:
play drum 2▾ for 0.25 beats	Play the drum sound.
	End of IF block.
↰	Keep checking.

Click the flag to test your code.

CUSTOMISE

• Make more drums by duplicating: Right-click a drum on the Stage and click **Duplicate**.

• Experiment with other sounds and images.

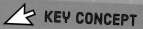 **KEY CONCEPT**

IF STATEMENT
An IF statement is used to perform a function or display information if something is proved true: if the drum is touched by the sprite, the drum is played.

> CATCH THE BUTTERFLY

Most computer games use a score to show you how well you have done. This game uses the score to track how many times the cat catches a butterfly. The score will be stored in a special part of the code called a variable. To make the game more realistic, the sprites will also use animation to make it look as if they are running or flying.

STEP I - PLANNING

When coding a more complex program, it's always worth thinking about how your program will work before you start. Many coders draw diagrams or pictures to help.

The arrow keys will move the cat sprite up, down, left or right.

The score is kept in a variable.

score `1`

The butterfly will fly around the stage, changing direction randomly by a few degrees at a time. We will also need to keep changing its picture to animate it.

If the cat catches the butterfly, then:
• Play a sound effect
• Increase the score
• Make the butterfly start again in a new random place.

Stop the game after 30 seconds.

Now the game is planned, we can turn the ideas into code.

STEP 2 - AT THE START

⇨ There are certain things the cat sprite needs to do each time the game starts. Add the following code so the sprite starts at the centre of the screen at half its size. Experiment with the size and starting co-ordinates by changing the x, y and % values (see page 8).

```
when  clicked
go to x:  0  y:  0
set size to  50  %
```

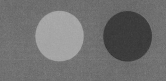

STEP 3 - MOVE RIGHT

⇨ Add this code to the cat sprite so it moves right when you press the right arrow key on your keyboard:

Code	Explanation
when **right arrow ▾** **key pressed**	Run the following code when the right arrow is pressed:
next costume	Change costume to show the cat in a different pose.
point in direction 90 ▾	Point the cat to the right.
move 10 **steps**	Move the cat 10 steps forward in its current direction.

STEP 4 - MOVE LEFT

⇨ Add this code to the cat sprite so it moves left when you press the left arrow key on your keyboard:

Code	Explanation
when **left arrow ▾** **key pressed**	Run the following code when the left arrow is pressed:
next costume	Change costume to show the cat in a different pose.
point in direction -90 ▾	Point the cat to the left.
move 10 **steps**	Move the cat 10 steps forward in its current direction.

STEP 5 - MOVE UP AND DOWN

⇨ Make the cat sprite move up and down when you press the up and down arrows by repeating the code used in steps 3 and 4, but altering the key pressed and the direction:

- To move up, point in direction 0
- To move down, point in direction 180.

Turn over to find out how to finish the game.

STEP 6 – KEEPING SCORE

⇨ To make a variable that can store the score, click the orange **Data** blocks and then click on **Make a Variable**.

⇨ Add the variable name as 'score'.

⇨ Click **OK**.

⇨ Drag the **set score to 0** block to the end of the code used in step 2. This will ensure that the starting score is always 0.

Data

Make a Variable

Make a List

Variable name: score |

⦿ For all sprites ○

set score ▾ to 0

CUSTOMISE

• Why not customise the game by using different sprites and backgrounds?

• Try a car chase, bats chasing ducks or a battle with angry dinosaurs.

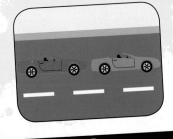

STEP 7 – SOMETHING TO CHASE

⇨ Add a sprite for the cat to chase by clicking the **Choose sprite from library** icon.

⇨ Select **Butterfly1**.

⇨ Click **OK**.

STEP 8 - BUTTERFLY CODE

⇨ We need the butterfly to move. If the computer chooses a random value, the butterfly's movement cannot be predicted. Drag the following code to the **Scripts Area**.

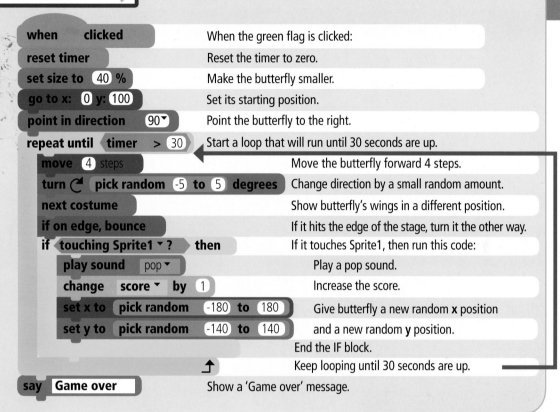

Code	Explanation
when clicked	When the green flag is clicked:
reset timer	Reset the timer to zero.
set size to 40 %	Make the butterfly smaller.
go to x: 0 y: 100	Set its starting position.
point in direction 90▾	Point the butterfly to the right.
repeat until timer > 30	Start a loop that will run until 30 seconds are up.
move 4 steps	Move the butterfly forward 4 steps.
turn ↻ pick random -5 to 5 degrees	Change direction by a small random amount.
next costume	Show butterfly's wings in a different position.
if on edge, bounce	If it hits the edge of the stage, turn it the other way.
if touching Sprite1 ▾ ? then	If it touches Sprite1, then run this code:
play sound pop ▾	Play a pop sound.
change score ▾ by 1	Increase the score.
set x to pick random -180 to 180	Give butterfly a new random **x** position
set y to pick random -140 to 140	and a new random **y** position.
	End the IF block.
↑	Keep looping until 30 seconds are up.
say Game over	Show a 'Game over' message.

STEP 9 - DRAW A BACKGROUND

⇨ Click the **Stage** icon in the **Sprites Pane**.

⇨ Click the **Backdrops** tab.

⇨ Select or draw a simple background.

 🚩 Enjoy playing your game!

 KEY CONCEPT

USING VARIABLES

Variables are special parts of a program that store information. In this game, the score is a variable. Variables can change as a program runs. The score in this game can go up or down. Variables have a name that is used to point to a part of the computer's memory. A value is then stored in that part of the memory.

❯ FLYING BIRD

This program uses more advanced maths to make a bird fly up and down at different speeds. To make the bird fly, we are going to use a variable to store the speed of the bird. By increasing the speed of the bird, it will look as though it is accelerating because of gravity. The bird will also use animation to flap its wings.

STEP 1 – ADD A NEW SPRITE

⇨ Remove the cat: right-click on the **Sprites Pane** and click **delete**.

⇨ Click the **Paint new sprite** icon.

STEP 2 – DRAW THE BIRD

⇨ The new sprite is going to be a bird. To make it look as though it is flying, we need to draw two costumes and animate them. Make the bird quite large so detail can be added. We can shrink it later.

⇨ In the **Costumes Area**, click on the **Rectangle** tool, choose the filled rectangle and pick a colour for the bird.

⇨ Draw a large body by clicking and dragging to the required size.

⇨ Add a rectangular head in a slightly darker colour.

⇨ Draw a small white square in the middle of the head, with a small black square in the bottom-right of the white square to make the eye.

⇨ Choose the colour orange and add two small rectangles for the beak.

STEP 3 – DUPLICATE IT

⇨ In the **New costume** area of the **Costumes Pane**, right-click on **costume1** and click **duplicate**. You should now see two costumes.

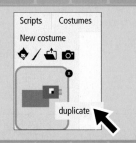

STEP 4 – DRAW THE WINGS

⇨ Click **costume1**. Use the **Rectangle** tool to draw dark green wings going up.

⇨ Click **costume2**. Now draw wings going down.

If you make a mistake when painting, click the Undo icon.

STEP 5 – MAKE THEM FLAP

⇨ Click the **Scripts** tab. Drag the following code into the **Scripts Area**; it will keep swapping the two costumes over:

when ⚑ clicked	When the green flag is clicked:
forever	Start a loop that will keep going forever
next costume	Swap to the next costume.
wait 0.1 secs	Wait for 0.1 seconds.
↰	End of the loop, go back to the start of the loop.

⚑ Run the code by clicking the green flag. Try changing the amount of time the program waits between changing costumes.

STEP 6 – MAKE YOUR VARIABLES

⇨ You will need two variables: one to keep score and one to store how fast the bird will be going up or down. Select the orange **Data** blocks.

⇨ Click on **Make a Variable** and name it 'score'.

⇨ Click **OK**.

⇨ Repeat this process for another variable called 'speed'.

STEP 7 – FLY AWAY!

⇨ Drag this code into the **Scripts Area**. It will make the bird fall down the screen and get slightly faster as it goes. Its wings should still be flapping from the code added in step 5.

when ⚑ clicked	When the green flag is clicked:
set score to 0	Start the score at 0.
set size to 30 %	Make the bird smaller.
go to x: 0 y: 0	Move the bird to the middle of the stage.
set speed to 0	Set the speed to 0.
repeat until	Start a repeat loop (we can add the 'until' condition later).
change speed by -0.15	Make the speed go down.
change y by speed	Change the 'y' value by the value stored in speed.
↰	Keep repeating.

⚑ Click the flag to test your code.

STEP 8 – KEY PRESS CODE

➪ Add the following code:

```
when space ▾ key pressed
change speed ▾ by 5
```

When the space key is pressed, the speed variable will go up by 5, making the bird move up gradually.

STEP 9 – ADD SOUND

➪ Click the **Sounds** tab.

➪ Select **Choose sound from library**.

➪ Click **bird**.

➪ Click **OK**.

➪ Drag a **play sound bird** block to the bottom of your code.

⚑ Try out your code. The bird should fly up when you press the space key and make a tweeting sound!

```
when space ▾ key pressed
change speed ▾ by 5
play sound bird ▾
```

STEP 10 – ADD AN OBSTACLE

➪ Now we need to add an obstacle for the bird to fly over. Click the **Paint new sprite** icon.

➪ Use the **Rectangle** tool to draw two large rectangles. There needs to be a big enough gap in the middle for the bird to fly through.

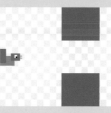

➪ Draw something simple to start with and add more detail later. The obstacle could look like a mountain, but it needs to be mainly one colour.

STEP 11 – MAKE IT MOVE

➪ Add the following code and then try it out. See if you can fly the bird through the gap in the obstacle.

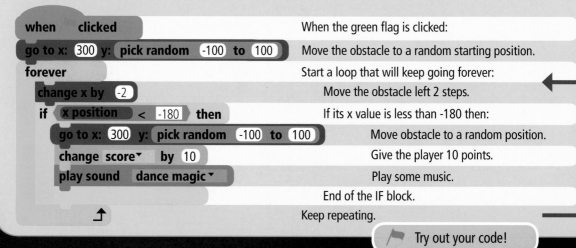

Code	Explanation
when ⚑ clicked	When the green flag is clicked:
go to x: 300 y: pick random -100 to 100	Move the obstacle to a random starting position.
forever	Start a loop that will keep going forever:
change x by -2	Move the obstacle left 2 steps.
if x position < -180 then	If its x value is less than -180 then:
go to x: 300 y: pick random -100 to 100	Move obstacle to a random position.
change score ▾ by 10	Give the player 10 points.
play sound dance magic ▾	Play some music.
	End of the IF block.
	Keep repeating.

⚑ Try out your code!

STEP 12 - STOP COLLISIONS

⇨ We need to make the game end when the bird hits the obstacle. Click on the bird sprite in the **Sprites Pane**. Find the step 7 code with the **repeat until** loop.

⇨ Drag in a **touching colour** block and set it to check for the colour of your obstacle. Click the actual obstacle in the **Stage** area of the screen to choose the colour.

⇨ Now, if the bird touches something that is the colour of your obstacle, it will drop out of the **repeat until** loop.

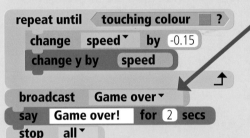

⇨ When the bird drops out of the repeat loop, the game is over and we need to:

• Broadcast 'Game over!' to tell other sprites that the game needs to stop.

• Tell the player the game is over using a say block.

• Stop all other code for the bird sprite.

STEP 13 - STOP EVERYTHING!

⇨ There is one more script we need to add to the obstacle sprite to make sure it stops too. Click on the obstacle in the **Sprites Pane** and add the following code:

| when I receive Game over ▾ | The code stops when another sprite broadcasts the 'Game over' message. |
| stop other scripts in sprite ▾ | Stop any other scripts that control the obstacle. |

STEP 14 - DRAW A BACKGROUND

⇨ Click the **Stage** icon in the **Sprites Pane**.

⇨ Click the **Backdrops** tab.

⇨ Keep the background simple. Draw a rectangle at the top and the bottom in the same colour as the obstacle. This will stop the bird flying too high or too low.

 **KEY CONCEPT**

USING VARIABLES TO REPRESENT GRAVITY

To create realistic and smooth acceleration, we increase the speed variable for every loop. Then, we change the **y** value of the bird by the figure stored in the speed variable.

 🚩 Now press the green flag to check your code and play your game!

› BASKETBALL CATCH

In the games we have made so far, there were only a couple of sprites. To create really exciting games, you need to have lots of sprites to make things challenging for the player. The best way to create multiple sprites is to clone them. In this game, the cat needs to catch multiple basketballs.

STEP I – PLANNING ▷

When coding a more complex program, it's always worth thinking about how your program will work before you start. Many coders draw diagrams or pictures to help.

The score is kept in a variable.

The timer is used to make the game stop after 30 seconds.

There are five basketballs created by a **repeat loop** that clones one basketball. They start in random places. Each ball moves down the **Stage** in a loop, as if it was falling. When it reaches the bottom of the **Stage**, the ball starts again in a random position.

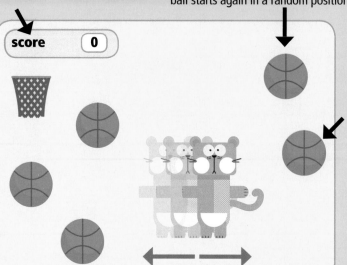

score [0]

If the cat catches a ball (use a **touch sensor** code block) then:

- increase the score
- play a sound effect
- make the ball start again in a random position.

Make the cat change direction when the arrow keys are pressed. Use animation to make it look as if it is running.

STEP 2 – CHOOSE A BACKGROUND ▷

⇨ Click the **Stage** icon in the **Sprites Pane**.

⇨ Click the **Choose backdrop from library** icon.

⇨ Click the **basketball-court1-b** image, or your own choice.

⇨ Click **OK**.

STEP 3 – CODE THE PLAYER

⇨ Click the **Sprite1** cat icon in the **Sprites Pane**, then click the **Scripts** tab.

⇨ To make the player start moving, add this code to the **Scripts Area**:

Code	Explanation
when ⚑ clicked	When the green flag is clicked:
set score ▾ to 0	Set the score to zero.
set size to 60 %	Make the cat much smaller.
go to x: 0 y: -128	Move it to the centre of the screen, near the bottom.
reset timer	Reset the timer, so we can have a time limit.
repeat until timer > 30	Repeat this code until the time limit is up (30 seconds for now):
move 5 steps	Move the cat five steps in its current direction.
next costume	Show its legs in a different position so it looks like it's running.
↰	Keep looping until the time is up.

For help making the score variable, see page 15.

⚑ Try out your code so far. The cat should shrink, then run off to the right of the screen.

STEP 4 – LEFT AND RIGHT

⇨ The repeat loop added at step 3 means that the cat will always be moving. This will give the game a bit more urgency and will make the game faster-paced. To make the cat move left and right, add the following code:

when left arrow ▾ key pressed
point in direction -90 ▾

When the left arrow key is pressed, the cat will point to the left.

when right arrow ▾ key pressed
point in direction 90 ▾

When the right arrow key is pressed, the cat will point to the right.

⚑ Try out your code so far.

STEP 5 – SOMETHING TO CATCH

⇨ Add a ball sprite for the cat to catch by clicking on the **Choose sprite from library** icon.

⇨ Select **Basketball** or one of the other balls.

⇨ Click **OK**.

STEP 6 – GET CLONING!

⇨ We have one ball, but we need more. To do this, we make a script that clones the ball. Cloning in Scratch means creating an exact copy of a sprite. Add the following code to the basketball to create five basketballs:

⇨ Remember, Scratch will clone everything about the sprite, including its **x** and **y** co-ordinates. A cloned sprite will be hidden behind its original sprite.

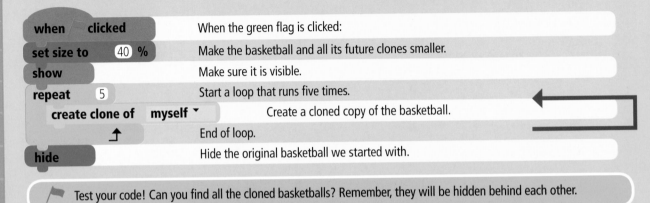

when clicked	When the green flag is clicked:
set size to 40 %	Make the basketball and all its future clones smaller.
show	Make sure it is visible.
repeat 5	Start a loop that runs five times.
create clone of myself	Create a cloned copy of the basketball.
↰	End of loop.
hide	Hide the original basketball we started with.

🏳 Test your code! Can you find all the cloned basketballs? Remember, they will be hidden behind each other.

STEP 7 – MOVE THE BALLS

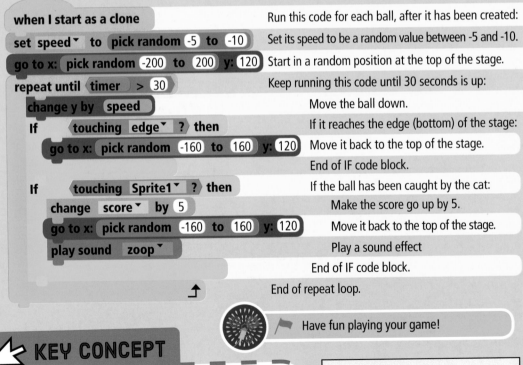

when I start as a clone	Run this code for each ball, after it has been created:
set speed to pick random -5 to -10	Set its speed to be a random value between -5 and -10.
go to x: pick random -200 to 200 y: 120	Start in a random position at the top of the stage.
repeat until timer > 30	Keep running this code until 30 seconds is up:
change y by speed	Move the ball down.
If touching edge ? then	If it reaches the edge (bottom) of the stage:
go to x: pick random -160 to 160 y: 120	Move it back to the top of the stage.
	End of IF code block.
If touching Sprite1 ? then	If the ball has been caught by the cat:
change score by 5	Make the score go up by 5.
go to x: pick random -160 to 160 y: 120	Move it back to the top of the stage.
play sound zoop	Play a sound effect
	End of IF code block.
↰	End of repeat loop.

🏳 Have fun playing your game!

Give each ball its own speed

In a game like this, with multiple cloned sprites, each clone needs to move in its own way, at its own speed. To make this happen, when you create the speed variable, click the button that says **For this sprite only**. This ensures each sprite has its own individual speed value.

➤ KEY CONCEPT

CLONES
The best way to create multiple sprites that all behave in the same way is to clone them.

Variable name: speed |

○ For all sprites ● For this sprite only

CUSTOMISE

• Why not try to make the game more challenging by adding more balls or making them move in slightly different directions?

• You could add another block of code that would pick a random direction for the ball to move in.

• Try making up your own catching game using completely different sprites and background images.

• Alternatively, why not try to add a tune that plays at the beginning and end of the game – or even during the game?

⇨ Why not add sound at the start of the game?

Make a gap in your code at the start, before the main game begins.

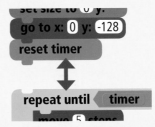

Drop in some **play note** code blocks in the gap. Choose an instrument to use.

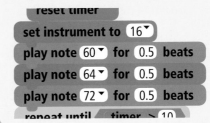

⇨ To add sound at the end:

play note 60 for 0.5 beats
play note 57 for 0.5 beats
play note 53 for 0.5 beats

Drop in some **play note** blocks after the main loop has finished and the time is up.

⇨ To add background sound to the whole game:

Add another **when green flag clicked** block and attach a **repeat until** block below it. Drop a **play sound until done** block inside the loop. Every time the sound finishes, it will start again – so your game will have a constant soundtrack!

› MUSICAL KEYBOARD

We are going to create a musical computer keyboard. By using the **set instrument** code block, the keyboard will be able to sound like a guitar, synthesiser or piano. Pressing different keys on the computer keyboard will play different musical notes. To avoid repeating all the code for each note, we will create our own blocks and define our own special play function.

STEP I – PLANNING

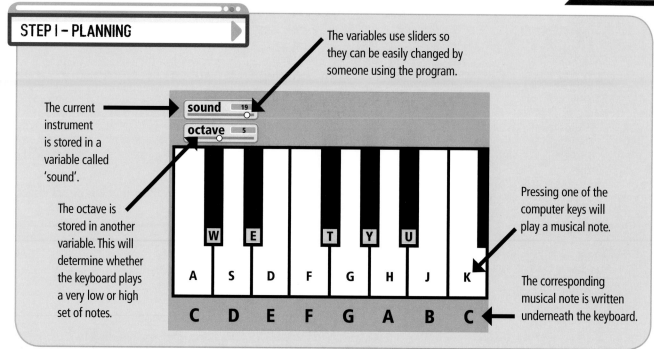

The variables use sliders so they can be easily changed by someone using the program.

The current instrument is stored in a variable called 'sound'.

The octave is stored in another variable. This will determine whether the keyboard plays a very low or high set of notes.

Pressing one of the computer keys will play a musical note.

The corresponding musical note is written underneath the keyboard.

STEP 2 – REMOVE THE CAT

⇨ Start by removing the cat sprite. Right-click on the cat sprite in the **Sprites Pane** and select **delete**.

STEP 3 – MAKE VARIABLES

⇨ Click the **Data** blocks and select **Make a Variable**. Call the variable 'sound', then make another variable called 'octave'.

⇨ Right-click on each variable at the top-left of the **Stage** and select **slider**.

⇨ Right-click on each variable again and choose **set slider min and max**. For 'sound', set the variable minimum as 1 and the maximum as 21. For 'octave', set the variable minimum as 2 and the maximum as 8. Moving the slider will change the value of the variable between these two values.

STEP 4 – ADD A NEW BLOCK ▶

⇨ Click the **More blocks** group and select **Make a Block**.

⇨ Type a name inside the purple block: 'play'.

⇨ Click **Options**.

⇨ Click **Add number input**.

⇨ Click **OK**.

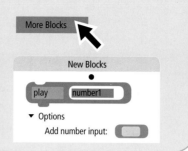

More Blocks

New Blocks

play   number1

▾ Options

Add number input:

STEP 5 – A NEW BLOCK ▶

define play number1

set instrument to   sound

play note octave * 12 + number1   for 0.5 beats

↑

The first part changes the pitch of the note that is played.

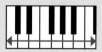

It is multiplied by 12 because there are 12 semitones in an octave.

Whenever the new play code block is used, the following code will run:

Set the musical instrument to the value of the sound variable.

Play a musical note. Drag number1 from the play block above.

The second part adds on the number that is sent to the function. The higher the number, the higher the pitch of the sound we hear.

STEP 6 – USE THE NEW PLAY BLOCK ▶

⇨ Add the following code:

when A ▾ key pressed

play 0

When the **A** key is pressed, run the function **play**.

when S ▾ key pressed

play 2

When the **S** key is pressed, run the **play** function with a value of 2.

when D ▾ key pressed

play 4

When the **D** key is pressed, run the **play** function with a value of 4.

⇨ Repeat step 6 and add code to make other keys run the 'play' function. Use the following values for each key: for **F** use a value of 5; for **G** use 7; for **H** use 9; for **J** use 11; for **K** use 12; for **W** use 1; for **E** use 3; for **T** use 6; for **Y** use 8 and for **U** use 10.

	F	G	H	J	K			W	E	T	Y	U
Play	5	7	9	11	12		Play	1	3	6	8	10

🚩 Test the code by clicking the green flag. Try pressing each of the A, S and D keys to play a simple tune.

◁ **KEY CONCEPT**

FUNCTIONS

As well as all the commands that are already in Scratch, we can add our own new blocks by combining them. Programmers call this writing your own functions.

If you create your own functions:

• you won't have to keep writing the same code

• your code will be easier for other people to understand.

> SPACE SHAPE ZAPPER

In this game, a number of shapes are falling down from space and need to be zapped by your player. The shapes will all be created as clones. The player will need to fire laser beams – which will also be created as clones.

STEP 1 – PLANNING

The score is kept in a variable. Two 'hidden' variables are also needed (un-tick them after creating them):

When the game is running we set **gameOn** to 1. When the laser is hit by a shape, it will be set to 0.

Speed stores the speed for each shape as it falls. (Tick **For this sprite only**).

A loop moves each shape down the screen. It also rotates as it falls.

When it reaches the bottom of the stage, the shape starts again in a random position at the top.

score   0

The player can fire a laser beam at the shapes by pressing the space bar. This will create a new clone of the laser beam.

If a shape is hit by a laser beam, the score will go up and the shape will go back to the top.

If the laser beam hits the shape, the game is over. A sound effect will be played and a message will say: Game Over!

GAME OVER

Make the laser change direction when the arrow keys are pressed.

STEP 2 – CHOOSE A BACKGROUND

⇨ Click the **Stage** icon in the **Sprites Pane**.

⇨ Click the **Choose backdrop from library** icon.

⇨ Click the **stars** image, or your own choice.

⇨ Click **OK**.

STEP 3 – MAKE THE LASER

⇨ Right-click the cat sprite and select **delete**.

⇨ Click the **Paint new sprite** icon.

⇨ In the **Costumes Pane**, select the **Rectangle** tool and choose the filled shape. Pick a colour for the laser. Draw the laser with three rectangles.

⇨ Click the **Set costume centre** icon. Carefully click the centre of the laser. This will make sure that the laser beam is fired from the centre of the laser.

STEP 4 – CODE THE GAME START

⇨ Go to the **Scripts Area** and add the following code to the laser:

Code	Explanation
when ⚑ clicked	When the green flag is clicked:
switch backdrop to stars ▾	Show the stars background.
set score ▾ to 0	Set the score to 0.
set gameOn ▾ to 1	Set the gameOn variable to 1.
set size to 20 %	Make the laser smaller.
go to x: 0 y: -145	Start the laser in the centre at the bottom.
repeat until gameOn = 0	Keep repeating until the gameOn variable is 0.
move 4 steps	Move the laser 4 pixels in the current direction.
↑	Keep looping.

Set up the 'score' and 'gameOn' variables (see page 14 for help on setting up variables). To stop the gameOn variable showing on screen, untick the box next to it.

 Now test your code.

STEP 5 – LASER MOVEMENT

⇨ To make the laser move left and right, add this code:

```
when left arrow ▾ key pressed
point in direction -90 ▾
```

```
when right arrow ▾ key pressed
point in direction 90 ▾
```

⇨ We need to stop the laser rotating when we change direction. Click the white **i** in the **Sprites Pane**. This shows and sets information about the sprite.

⇨ Click on the left-right arrow in the rotation style. Click the white arrow in the blue circle when you have finished.

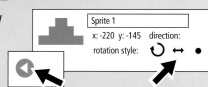

STEP 6 – MAKE A LASER BEAM

⇨ Click the **Paint new sprite** icon.

⇨ Use the **Rectangle** tool to make a laser beam that shoots up the stage.

⇨ Click the **Set costume centre** button and click on the centre of the laser beam.

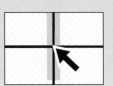

STEP 7 – CODE THE LASER

⇨ Add the following three pieces of code to the **Scripts Area**:

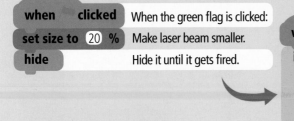

when clicked	When the green flag is clicked:
set size to 20 %	Make laser beam smaller.
hide	Hide it until it gets fired.

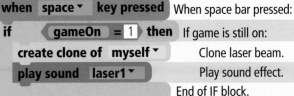

when space ▼ key pressed	When space bar pressed:
if gameOn = 1 then	If game is still on:
create clone of myself ▼	Clone laser beam.
play sound laser1 ▼	Play sound effect.
	End of IF block.

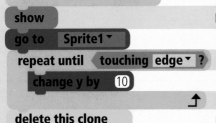

when I start as a clone	When laser beam is cloned:
show	Make sure it's visible.
go to Sprite1 ▼	Move laser beam to the laser.
repeat until touching edge ▼ ?	Loop until it gets to the top.
change y by 10	Move laser beam up.
↰	Keep repeating.
delete this clone	Delete laser beam clone.

STEP 8 – MAKE THE SHAPE

⇨ Click the **Paint new sprite** icon.

⇨ Use the **Rectangle** tool to make a simple shape.

⇨ Click the **Set costume centre** button and click on the centre of the shape.

STEP 9 – STARTING POSITIONS

⇨ We will need to set the position of the shape at several different points in the program. To avoid repeating code, we will need to define a function.

⇨ When you create the **speed** variable, set it **For this sprite only**. This means each shape has its own speed. Click on the **Scripts** tab and add the following:

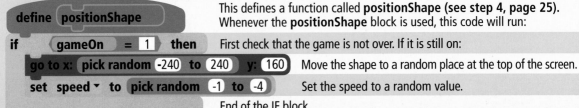

define positionShape	This defines a function called **positionShape (see step 4, page 25)**. Whenever the **positionShape** block is used, this code will run:
if gameOn = 1 then	First check that the game is not over. If it is still on:
go to x: pick random -240 to 240 y: 160	Move the shape to a random place at the top of the screen.
set speed ▼ to pick random -1 to -4	Set the speed to a random value.
	End of the IF block.

STEP 10 - MOVING THE SHAPES

➡ Make a function to move a shape by adding the following code:

```
define moveShape
```
This code defines a function called **moveShape**.
When the **moveShape** block is used, the following code will run:

```
repeat until  touching Sprite1 ▼ ?
```
Keep looping the following code until the laser beam hits the shape.

```
    turn ↻ speed degrees
```
Rotate the shape to the right by the value stored in 'speed'.

```
    change y by speed
```
Move the shape down by the value stored in 'speed'.

```
    if  touching edge ▼ ?  then
```
If the shape hits the edge of the stage:

```
        positionShape
```
Run the function that positions the shape.

End of the IF block.

```
    if  touching Sprite3 ▼ ?  then
```
If the shape has been hit by a laser beam:

```
        change score ▼ by 1
```
Make the score go up by 1.

```
        positionShape
```
Run the code that positions the shape.

```
        play sound laser2 ▼
```
Play a sound effect.

End of the IF block.

Keep looping.

```
set gameOn ▼ to 0
```
Set the variable 'gameOn' to 0. This signals to the other sprites that the game is over.

STEP 11 - START CLONING

➡ Add the following two groups of code to make all the cloned shapes:

```
when ⚑ clicked
```
When the green flag is clicked:

```
set size to 10 %
```
Shrink the original shape.

```
show
```
Make sure it is visible.

```
repeat 10
```
Repeat 10 times for 10 clones.

```
    change clone of myself ▼
```
Clone the shape.

Keep repeating.

```
hide
```
Now hide the original shape.

```
when I start as a clone
positionShape
moveShape
```

Each time a shape is cloned, it will be in the same place. Adding the **positionShape** block will put it in a random place. The **moveShape** block will make the shape move down the screen.

STEP 12 - FINAL BACKDROP

➡ Play some music and show 'Game Over!' by clicking the laser in the **Sprites Pane** and adding this code to the bottom of the **repeat until** block from step 4:

```
play sound dance slow mo ▼
say Game Over!
```

 ⚑ Have fun playing your game!

〈29〉

GLOSSARY

ALGORITHM Rules or steps followed to do something.

ANIMATION Making an image seem to move.

BACKDROP The stationary background picture behind any sprites.

BROADCASTING How a sprite can share a message with other sprites.

BUG An error in a program that stops it working properly.

CLONE An identical copy of a sprite.

CODE BLOCK A draggable instruction icon used in Scratch.

COMMAND A special word that tells a computer to do something.

CONDITIONAL A block of code that only runs if something is true.

CO-ORDINATES The position of a sprite using **x** and **y** values to describe how far across, and up or down, it is from the centre of the stage.

COSTUME An image shown on a sprite. Multiple costumes are used in Scratch to create animations.

DEBUG To remove bugs (or errors) from a program.

DEGREES The units used to measure angles.

DUPLICATE A copy of something, such as a sprite.

FUNCTION Several commands that in combination do something.

ICON A small clickable image on a computer.

LOOP Repeating one or more commands a number of times.

OCTAVE A series of eight notes in music.

PITCH How high or low a musical note is.

PIXEL A tiny dot on a screen. Lots of pixels can make one whole image.

RANDOM A number or value that can't be predicted.

RIGHT-CLICK Clicking the right mouse button on a sprite or icon.

SEQUENCE Commands that are run one after another in order.

SPRITE An object with a picture on it that moves around the stage, such as the cat.

STAGE The place in Scratch that sprites move around on.

STEPS Small movements made by sprites.

VARIABLE A value that can change, used to store information in a program.

CHECKLIST

If you can't find the blocks you need when coding:

⇨ Use the colours to look in the right group

⇨ Scroll through all the blocks

⇨ Check drop-down menus in similar blocks.

Remember, if you:

⇨ Can't find **set variable**? You need to make it first!

⇨ Can't find a particular sound? You need to get it from the library first!

⇨ Can't find any **Move** blocks? Select the **Stage**, then click on the icon you want to add code to.

BUGS AND DEBUGGING

When you find your code isn't working as expected, stop and look through each command you have put in. Some things to check:

⇨ Join blocks properly.

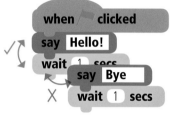

```
when   clicked
say  Hello!
wait  1  secs
    say  Bye
    wait  1  secs
```
✓
✗

⇨ Sprites too big or too small? Use the **set size** block to choose how big sprites are. Change the percentage value to make them fit properly.

⇨ Select sprites before adding code.

⇨ Are your sprites rotating or flipping when you don't want them to? Click on the 'i' on the sprites icon and select the double arrow on the rotation style.

⇨ Which co-ordinate: x or y? Don't mix them up.

⇨ Reset things at the start.

```
when   clicked
show
```

If you hide shapes during your code, make sure you add a show block at the start.

⇨ Right colour, wrong code? Be precise, many code blocks look very similar, but do completely different things.

⇨ Set or change?

```
set  score ▾  to  1
```

```
change  score ▾  by  1
```

Give each variable a starting value with the **set** command. Use the **change** block to make it go up or down.

⇨ Position variables and values carefully.

```
change  y  by  speed
```
✓

Don't type in variable names or drop them on top of blocks. Drag them until a circle appears. The value block will then snap into place.

⇨ Choose which sprites can use a variable. If you want to give cloned sprites different speeds, choose **For this sprite only** when creating them.

TIPS TO REDUCE BUGS

⇨ If you are making your own program, spend time planning it before you start.

⇨ Practise debugging! Make a very short program and get a friend to change one block only while you aren't looking. Can you fix it?

⇨ When things are working properly, spend time looking through your code so you understand each line. To be good at debugging, you need to understand what each code block does and how your code works.

INDEX

First published in Great Britain in 2017 by Wayland

Text copyright © ICT Apps Ltd, 2017
Art and design copyright © Hodder and Stoughton Limited, 2017

Editor: Liza Miller
Freelance editor: Hayley Fairhead
Designer: Peter Clayman
Illustrator: Ladiebirdy

ISBN: 978 1 5263 0102 4
10 9 8 7 6 5 4 3 2 1

Wayland
An imprint of
Hachette Children's Group
Part of Hodder & Stoughton
Carmelite House
50 Victoria Embankment
London EC4Y 0DZ

An Hachette UK Company
www.hachette.co.uk
www.hachettechildrens.co.uk

Printed in China

The website addresses (URLs) included in this book were valid at the time of going to press. However, it is possible that contents or addresses may have changed since the publication of this book. No responsibility for any such changes can be accepted by either the author or the Publisher.

E-safety
Children will need access to the internet for most of the activities in this book. Parents or teachers should supervise this and discuss staying safe online with children.